Burning Desire

Obadiah/Malachi

GW00641887

by
Phillip D. Jensen
&
Richard Pulley

Burning Desire
© Matthias Media 1998

Matthias Media
(St Matthias Press Ltd. ACN 067 558 365)
PO Box 225
Kingsford NSW 2032
Australia
Telephone: (02) 9663 1478; international: +61-2-9663-1478
Facsimile: (02) 9663 3265; international: +61-2-9663-3265
Email: info@matthiasmedia.com.au
Internet: www.matthiasmedia.com.au

Matthias Media (USA)
Telephone: 724 964 8152; international: +1-724-964-8152
Facsimile: 724 964 8166; international: +1-724-964-8166
Email: sales@matthiasmedia.com
Internet: www.matthiasmedia.com

ISBN 978 1 876326 11 1

Typesetting and design by Lankshear Design Pty Ltd.

Contents

How to make the most of these studies

1. What is an Interactive Bible Study?

These 'interactive' Bible studies are a bit like a guided tour of a famous city. The studies will take you on a tour through Obadiah and Malachi, pointing out things along the way, filling in background details, and suggesting avenues for further exploration. But there is also time for you to do some sightseeing of your own—to wander off, have a good look for yourself, and form your own conclusions.

In other words, we have designed these studies to fall halfway between a sermon and a set of unadorned Bible study questions. We want to provide stimulation and input and point you in the right direction, while leaving you to do a lot of the exploration and discovery yourself.

We hope that these studies will stimulate lots of 'interaction'—interaction with the Bible, with the things we've written, with your own current thoughts and attitudes, with other people as you discuss them, and with God as you talk to him about it all.

2. The format

Each study contains sections of text to introduce, summarize, suggest and provoke. We've left plenty of room in the margins for you to jot comments and questions as you read.

Interspersed throughout the text are three types of 'interaction', each with its own symbol:

For starters

Questions to break the ice and get you thinking.

Investigate

Questions to help you investigate key parts of the Bible.

Think it through

Questions to help you think through the implications of your discoveries and write down your own thoughts and reactions.

When you come to one of these symbols, you'll know that it's time to do some work of your own.

3. Suggestions for individual study

- Before you begin, pray that God would open your eyes to what he is saying in Obadiah and Malachi and give you the spiritual strength to do something about it. You may be spurred to pray again at the end of the study.
- Work through the study, following the directions as you go. Write in the spaces provided.
- Resist the temptation to skip over the *Think it through* sections. It is important to think about the sections of text (rather than just accepting them as true) and to ponder the implications for your life. Writing these things down is a very valuable way to get your thoughts working.
- Take what opportunities you can to talk to others about what you've learnt.

4. Suggestions for group study

- Much of the above applies to group study as well. The studies are suitable for structured Bible study or cell groups, as well as for more informal pairs and triplets. Get together with a friend/s and work through them at your own pace. You don't need the formal structure of a 'group' to gain maximum benefit.
- It is *vital* that group members work through the study themselves *before* the group meets. The group discussion can take place comfortably in an hour (depending on how side-tracked you get!), but only if all the members have done the work and are familiar with the material.
- Spend most of the group time discussing the 'interactive' sections—*Investigate* and *Think it through*. Reading all the text together will take too long and should be unnecessary if the group members have done their preparation. You may wish to underline and read aloud particular paragraphs or sections of text that you think are important.
- The role of the group leader is to direct the course of the discussion and to try to draw the threads together at the end. This will mean a little extra preparation—underlining important sections of text to emphasize, working out which questions are worth concentrating on, and being sure of the main thrust of the study. Leaders will also probably want to work out approximately how long they'd like to spend on each part.
- We haven't included an 'answer guide' to the questions in the studies. This is a deliberate move. We want to give you a guided tour, not a lecture. There is more than enough in the text we have written and the questions we have asked to point you in what we think is the right direction. The rest is up to you.

Brothers divided

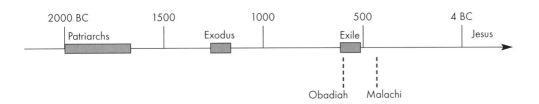

Success and failure

A few years after a war has ended, it becomes pretty obvious who won. The victors build great monuments to their achievements to show off their power to all around them. Those who were defeated bear the scars of their ruin, and anyone with their eyes open can observe their failure.

Such was the condition of Jerusalem in the 6th century B.C. After 500 years in the land that God had promised to Jacob's descendants, Jerusalem was conquered by Nebuchadnezzar and the Babylonians, and its inhabitants carried away in chains. In contrast, Babylon was a great city, proud of its Hanging Gardens, one of the seven wonders of the ancient world, and symbolic of its wealth, significance and power. The city reeked of success, just as Jerusalem reeked of failure.

Obadiah has his vision not long after Jerusalem has been taken into exile. God's people were friendless and desperate. By the rivers of Babylon, they wept. But not everyone was sorry to see the descendants of Jacob weeping in exile: the Edomites, who lived in the mountainous countryside to the south-east of Judah, took some pleasure in their downfall.

To find out why, we need to go back to the beginning of the Bible and the early promises of God to Abraham and his children.

Investigate

Work quickly through these passages and questions. Try not to get distracted by details. If you are in a group, it might be best to split the passages among group members, to save time.

Read Genesis 15.
1. What promises does God give to Abraham (Abram)? When will these promises come to fruition?

Read Genesis 25:19-34.
2. The "first-born" would inherit the largest portion of his father's estate. Given God's promises to Abraham, what did Esau stand to inherit?

3. How did Esau despise his birthright?

Read Numbers 20:14-21. Having been led out of captivity in Egypt, the Israelites are wandering in the wilderness. This passage provides some background to the kind of relationship that developed between Edom (Esau's descendants) and Israel (Jacob's descendants).

4. How would you describe Israel's request to Edom?

Reasonable

5. How would you describe Edom's reply?

Unreasonable.
Also turning his people against God.
Not very brotherly

A future inheritance

A breakdown of friendship between two brothers over an inheritance had, over time, developed into a stand-off between two nations. By satisfying himself in the here and now, Esau had given up the great promises that God had made to his grandfather, Abraham. As we saw, these promises extended far into the future —he would be given numerous descendants, a land of his own and triumph over his enemies. Esau gave up all of this for a bowl of stew and a hunk of bread. (In Genesis 27, the dying Isaac formally transferred his blessing to Jacob.)

The Edomites proved to have long memories and remained bitter towards the descendants of Jacob, right up to the time they were invaded by Nebuchadnezzar. Unfortunately for Edom, God also remembered the bitter treatment they had given his people, Israel. Obadiah's words of prophecy are directed against this wayward nation. We turn to these words now.

Investigate

Read Obadiah.

1. The Edomites seem proud and confident. From verses 1-9, why might they have had such confidence?

2. How does Obadiah describe the way the Edomites treated Israel when they were invaded by the Babylonians (vv. 10-14)?

3. What is to be the fate of Edom?

The sin of Edom

The city of Petra was probably typical of Edomite cities. Known to us today, the city was carved into the rock of a cliff-face, up in the mountainous areas of Edom. What better place to put a city! How do you lay siege to a city that you can't easily surround or access?

The Edomites thought their city was secure and unconquerable, and that they had powerful allies. On the contrary, Edom's pride was part of their sin, and their "wisdom" was of no consequence. Their pride would deceive them and their allies would be revealed as their enemies.

However, God wasn't primarily judging their pride, but their brotherly violence. Even back in the days of Moses, as we read in Numbers 20, Edom did nothing to help their relatives in their hour of need. They sent an army to chase them away. In the times of Obadiah, they did even worse. The saying is "Blood is thicker than water", but the Edomites spilt that blood. They sided with the pagans against their own brothers, seizing their wealth and cutting down those fleeing the destruction. Edom's great sin was ignoring its brotherly obligations.

Obadiah's vision saw Edom's sin and Edom's judgement. Yes, it would come, and it would be so terrible that nothing would be left of Edom. God would have his retribution for what had been done to Israel.

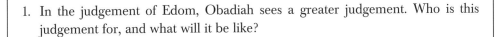

Investigate
Read Obadiah 15-21.

1. In the judgement of Edom, Obadiah sees a greater judgement. Who is this judgement for, and what will it be like?

2. What future does Obadiah see for Israel?

3. What do these passages tell us about how this future eventuates?

- Luke 2:25, 28-32

- Mark 1:15

- Revelation 11:15-18

The Kingdom of God

In the judgement of Edom, Obadiah sees the judgement of all the nations of the world who rise up against God. At the same time, we see God's burning desire for the people of his inheritance. God's holy city will be delivered, and his people will reclaim the promised land (the lands of the Philistines, Zarephath, Gilead and the Negev are found west, north, east and south of the promised land, hence representing the entire land).

Obadiah's message is consistent with the rest of the prophets. The day of the Lord is coming, when God's people will be saved and God's enemies destroyed. When Jesus came to earth, he announced the coming of the kingdom of God—the same kingdom that Obadiah foresaw. Yet this kingdom was even greater than that which Obadiah prophesied. The kingdom extends beyond any physical borders into the very presence of God. Those who are in Christ inherit the promises of Abraham, Isaac and Jacob. We inherit eternal life in the presence of God!

However, there are some who say that this future inheritance is of no use to them. Instead of living by faith, they live like Esau, grabbing what they can now—and in the process surrendering their inheritance. What use are such things if their cost is eternal life?

Think it through

1. Is there anything which you desire so much now that you would be tempted to give up your spiritual inheritance to have it?

2. How can you avoid falling into the trap of Esau?

3. Jesus tells us not to worry about what we will eat or wear, but to seek first the kingdom of God and his righteousness. What practical changes do you need to make in your life to do this?

    Phil 4 v 6

4. What message does Obadiah have for those who mock and oppose God's people today?

What love is this?

For starters

Have you ever questioned whether God really loves you?

How have you loved us?

Where is the evidence that God is in fact looking after us?

This question is literally as old as Malachi. From the time of Obadiah and the exile, we now jump forward about 150 years (see the timeline in the first study). Despite the odds, Israel has been saved from slavery. The Babylonians were conquered and the Persian King Cyrus decreed that the Israelites could return home and rebuild. Seventy years of exile were over.

God had promised much. Obadiah, as well as other prophets such as Isaiah and Ezekiel, had predicted that the people of God would be delivered from oppression, and that God would usher in a mighty kingdom that would last forever. These huge expectations, however, had not yet eventuated. Life was difficult, as crops failed and the neighbouring nations harassed God's people.

The prophecy of Malachi, whose name means "my messenger",

consists of a series of arguments with God. The first argument was that of a nation that felt itself to be the victim. "How have you loved us?", they asked. What have we got to show for it? How come we're in the mess that we're in?

God answers their question through Malachi, and, strangely enough, the answer again takes us back to Jacob and Esau. You will recall from study 1 that these twin brothers were the grandchildren of Abraham and therefore heirs of God's promises. Esau sold his birthright to Jacob for a single meal, and so God's promises transferred to Jacob, even though he was not the eldest son.

We now turn back to the story of their birth—and that stew—for some further insights into the nations that derived from this incident.

Investigate
Read Genesis 25:19-34.

1. What three things does the Lord tell Rebekah will occur to her twin sons?

   i.

   ii.

   iii.

2. What do we know so far about how these three things were brought about?

Read Malachi 1:1-5.

3. What became of the inheritance of the Edomites? What prospects are there for the future?

4. "I have loved you", says the Lord. How has the Lord shown his love for the Israelites?

Jacob and Esau, Israel and Edom

God promised Rebekah that her two sons would be the forefathers of two nations but, contrary to usual practice, the older would serve the younger (Gen 25:23). It was God's choice that one would be stronger than the other, and that they would be separated. Esau's negligent actions in handing over his birthright (and therefore his inheritance) indicated the initial outworking of this promise. We found in the previous study that the Edomites were never brotherly—there was much hostility directed towards Jacob's descendants.

The opening verses of Malachi seem rather extreme: the Lord contrasts his love for Israel with his hate for Esau. This was a common literary device in Hebrew, a way of making a radical statement as clear as possible. Jesus uses a similarly extreme expression in Luke 14:26 when he tells his would-be disciples that "if anyone comes to me and does not hate his father and mother, his wife and children, his brothers and sisters—yes, even his own life—he cannot be my disciple". As Malachi's prophecy begins, we are in no doubt as to how much God has loved the Israelites. The nation chosen by God was Israel, not Edom. Israel was taken into slavery, yet they have now returned from Babylon. For the Edomites, their inheritance has been left to the desert jackals, and any attempt that they may make to rebuild will be demolished by the Lord.

We are also given an insight into God's greatness (v. 5). Not only will Israel be blessed, but God's judgement on Edom will be seen beyond the borders of Israel. His protection of his chosen people, and the destruction of their enemies, will testify to all the nations that Israel's God is great.

This testimony has resonated down the centuries, preserved for us in Scripture. Four centuries after Malachi, the apostle Paul considered God's love for Jacob over Esau and explained how God has continued to demonstrate his love for his people in accordance with his promise.

Investigate

Read Romans 9:1-16.

1. Summarize Paul's concern in verses 1-7.

2. What two things did God tell Abraham (vv. 6-9)?

3. According to what criteria did God choose some of Abraham's descendants over others?

4. What does Paul conclude regarding God's children from these words and events?

5. How does this explain what Paul observed in his day, when many Israelites became Christians, and many did not?

God has spoken his word, which will not fail, and has not failed. The word was that the sons of Abraham would be the sons of special promise and election, and that Gentiles—those who weren't physically of the nation Israel—would also be saved through Israel. God's greatness was demonstrated both within Israel and outside it, as some Jews were converted while other Israelites-by-birth surrendered their birthright and rejected the gospel.

Not all of Abraham's physical descendants were true descendants of Abraham, but those who were inherited—namely that God would protect and cherish his people, and pour out his wrath upon their enemies. Christian believers have this same confidence, that nothing can put us outside this inheritance. It is expressed beautifully in Romans 8:37-39:

… we are more than conquerors through him who loved us. For I am convinced that neither death nor life, neither angels nor demons, neither the present nor the future, nor any powers, neither height nor depth, nor anything else in all creation, will be able to separate us from the love of God that is in Christ Jesus our Lord.

We can be confident that God will bring justice, but let us be patient. We ought to desire righteousness and remember what happened to Edom. Those who reject God will suffer his wrath in due course, because God is the Sovereign Lord of not only his chosen people, but the whole world.

Think it through

1. Are you a true child of Abraham? How is it that you know of God's love for you?

2. What sort of reaction do you have towards people who are opposed to God? What sort of reaction do you think you *ought* to have?

3. Todd and Murray have been discussing predestination. Todd finds it hard to believe that a loving God could choose for himself some people and not others. Murray is at a loss to know what to say to him. From what we have learnt in this study, what ideas could you offer to Murray?

Hallowed be your name

When pop diva Kylie Minogue rose to fame, she met a mixed reaction from Kylies around the world. Those who loved her music no doubt relished the connection with a famous performer; those who were less impressed knew that they had years of persecution ahead of them.

We attach a great deal of significance to our name, even though most of us don't choose it for ourselves. It comes to represent us— it's like a badge for our personality, our history and our values. Our reputation is tied up with our name (usually, our family name) such that we can talk about "blackening a name" or "upholding a name". In either case, the future of all those attached with the name is at stake.

God's name is similarly important to him because it represents his reputation and honour. In Malachi 1:6, God accuses Israel of betraying his name. As their father and master, where was the respect and honour due to him? And of all the people who should honour the name of Yahweh, surely the priests of Yahweh would be first among them.

Although God had not destroyed the Israelites as he did the Edomites, he was not happy with them.

Investigate

Read Deuteronomy 15:19-23, 17:1.

1. What sort of sacrifice does God require?

2. What is God's reaction to an imperfect sacrifice?

Read Malachi 1:6-14.

3. In what ways do the priests show disrespect for God's name?

4. Why is God not pleased with the sacrifices they give?

5. God's disgust with the "worship" of the Israelite priests moves him to make an astonishing statement in verses 10-11. What does he say, and what makes it so remarkable?

The nature of the offence

The Law of God was very clear in its requirements. To be an acceptable sacrifice, an animal had to be perfect. After all, to offer a diseased animal is no sacrifice at all. In breaking this law, the priests of Israel showed contempt for Yahweh. Today, when we do something illegal, we don't see it as an offence against any particular person; we are simply 'breaking the law'. But the law of Israel was the law of God himself. Rejecting that law meant rejecting God.

By offering what God had forbidden to be offered, the priests were rejecting God and showing contempt for him. They didn't even want to make the sacrifices, but described serving God as a burden (v. 13). Consider for a moment the hypocrisy and irony of making offerings to God of a type that is detestable to him, and without having your heart in it! God would rather that the temple be closed than endure their begrudging disrespect at the altar.

And yet there is the hint in verse 11 that in the future *the nations* will offer pleasing sacrifices to God. Pagans with no relationship to God whatsoever will end up pleasing God, while his own people cannot. How could this be so? We'll come to that in time.

Investigate

Read Malachi 2:1-9.

1. Levi and his descendants were set apart by God to be his priests. What does the passage tell us about the nature of a true priest of Yahweh?

2. In what ways have the priests of Malachi's time violated their covenant with God?

3. Malachi uses vivid language to describe the fate of the priests. What has happened to them, and what will happen, if they continue to bring dishonour to the name of God?

4. Why is God admonishing the priests?

The future of the priests

God had established a contract with Levi and his descendants to bring honour to his name. However the state of the priesthood which Malachi spoke against bore little relation to the one God had envisaged. Levites were to administer the truth of God to his people, as "messengers of the LORD Almighty" (Mal 2:7). But these priests showed partiality in matters of the law, and caused people to stumble by their teaching. They were wolves in sheep's clothing; they were false teachers. They fully deserve the gruesome humiliation which Malachi describes.

In the New Testament, all Christians are priests. We have one High Priest, Jesus Christ, who offered the one sacrifice for all time (Heb 7-10), but all Christians are priests in the sense that we are to be ministers of the word of God and mediators through prayer. We bear witness to the holy name of God, as these Scriptures testify:

> [Y]ou are a chosen people, a royal priesthood, a holy nation, a people belonging to God, that you may declare the praises of him who called you out of darkness into his wonderful light. (1 Pet 2:9)

> To him who loves us and has freed us from our sins by his blood, and has made us to be a kingdom and priests to serve his God and Father—to him be glory and power for ever and ever! Amen. (Rev 1:5-6)

How to be truly religious

If there was ever an official or authentic religion of God, then the appointed Levitical priesthood had to be it. And yet when they broke his law and taught in error, they were neither his priests nor his people. They may have been of the right lineage, but they weren't his priests.

God's word cannot be institutionalized. God's truth is truth no matter who speaks it, and it sits loosely with organized religion. Jesus rebuked his apostles for trying to stop others acting in the name of Jesus (Mark 9:38-39). The priests of Levi probably imagined that they were indispensable, but God would demonstrate his holiness by accepting the sacrifices of pagans instead. Eventually, through the gospel, he would equip Gentiles ("the nations" of Malachi 1:11) to be his messengers. All who walk in the righteousness that comes from Christ would "declare the praises of him who called [us] out of darkness into his wonderful light." These are the ones who honour the name of the Lord.

Think it through

1. In what ways do we offer God "defiled sacrifices"?

2. What would be a perfect sacrifice for Christians to make (see Rom 12:1-2)?

3. What has Malachi taught us about what it means to be truly religious? (See also Jas 1:26-27.)

4. What steps can we take to preserve the knowledge of God (Mal 2:7)?

5. Stephen has been a Christian for ten years, has a minor speech impediment, and has been Sunday School Superintendent for 12 months. Walter has been a parish Councillor for 25 years, oversees the Parish fund-raising, and is a polished public speaker. Both men are interested in preaching at your evening youth service. What criteria will you use to decide who is most suited to the task?

Breaking faith

It's hard to talk about divorce. Many of us know it close to hand, and it may be almost impossible to discuss it without bringing complex emotions to the surface. It is one of the most painful and pervasive social issues of our time, and it's also one of the most personal. We would prefer to avoid raising it.

However, the warning of the last study, where the priests were condemned for showing partiality in matters of the law (Mal 2:9), is still ringing in our ears so that when God says "I hate divorce" (Mal 2:16), we cannot leave the matter to one side.* We need to understand the warnings of Scripture about breaking faith, and then heed them. It's a difficult task, but one which we must try to do, in prayer, humility, and with an eye open to those of our Christian brothers and sisters around us for whom this subject will be very relevant indeed.

The meaning of faith

Malachi 2 is about keeping, or breaking, faith. Much of the Old Testament calls upon the nation of Israel (and each Israelite) to be faithful to God. The opposite of faithfulness is to break faith. Verse 10 is a key verse: "Have we not all one Father? Did not one God create us? Why do we profane the covenant of our fathers by breaking faith with one another?"

The word 'faith' has a diverse history among Christians. It has been used and misused for centuries. Commonly, people think of faith as a belief which cannot be proved. It's a kind of irrational

---

* Some versions (e.g. ESV) translate this verse somewhat differently, but God's condemnation of the faithlessness of divorce remains clear.

belief that's against the evidence—a leap in the dark. Faith in God is sometimes held to be the best we can do to 'know God' when in fact there is no way to be sure that we really know him at all.

But this is not at all the way the Bible writers understand faith. To them, faith is about an agreement—a covenant. It represents the clear understanding between two parties of the kind of relationship they have. It isn't a hidden or mysterious thing. The deal is on the table, for everyone to see.

We make 'covenants' with each other all the time. If I agree to give you a lift home after church, then we have a covenant. It is understood that I will let you know when I am about to leave, and that you won't disappear with someone else (at least not without notifying me). I might even give you the car keys as a sign of our covenant. By and large, biblical covenants operate in the same way. They involve making promises and having an obligation of loyalty to the agreement. They work on the basis of faith—the faithfulness of one party to keep the promise they made, and the faith of the other party to trust that the promise will be kept. If we are unfaithful to the promises we make, we have broken faith.

Investigate
Read Malachi 2:10-16.

1. Summarize the main issue this passage is addressing.

2. How do the people of Judah demonstrate their involvement in the religious life of the nation?

3. In verse 13, the people of Judah cry out to the Lord because their offerings are rejected. Why does God ignore their sacrifices?

4. In what way have the Israelites broken faith?

5. Why is what Judah and Israel have done considered to be "breaking the covenant" (vv. 14-15)?

The people of Judah were involved in false religion. They brought sacrifices to the altar, and yet in their marriages they revealed their unfaithfulness. They wanted to participate in the religion of the Lord their God, while at the same time denying the distinctiveness of their nation and their God by inter-marrying with foreigners who worshipped other gods. Even though they made a covenant with the wife of their youth, they showed that they were unfaithful to their word, and broke faith. Why is this so serious? To understand that, we need to look at marriage from God's perspective.

Marriage is a covenant

When we enter into a marriage, we are making promises for the future. At the time of marriage, we are bursting with love for our spouse, and promises seem easy to make. But in most Christian marriage services, we are asked if we will love them in the future—when beauty and youth have faded, when sickness and hardship have come. The Beatles had the right question when they sang, "Will you still need me, will you still feed me when I'm 64?"

When we say "I will", we are making a covenant with our spouse to love each other until death brings separation. Our responsibility is to be faithful to our promise and to keep our word. We also need to have faith in our partner, that they will be a person of their word.

Marriage, therefore, is a contract between two people which extends into the future. However, in Scripture, it is even more than that.

Investigate
Read Ephesians 5:21-33.

1. How is a husband to live inside a marriage relationship?

2. How is a wife to live inside a marriage relationship?

3. How does God's pattern for us in marriage help us to understand what Christ is like and how he relates to his people?

4. How does Christ and his relationship to his people help us understand marriage? How do you see this reflected in Malachi 2?

5. From Malachi 2, what is God's purpose in creating marriage?

Judah's unfaithfulness

Malachi describes marriage as two being made one, for the purpose of "godly offspring". There are echoes here of Genesis 2, where two are made from one and are in complete unity ("bone of my bones and flesh of my flesh"). And it is this unity and purity which produces godly offspring. In the context of Malachi, this means children who will grow up to worship and serve Yahweh and not some foreign god. By breaking faith with the wife of their youth, and marrying a foreign wife, the men of Judah had put all this in jeopardy.

In fact, they had been doubly unfaithful. First, they had broken faith with their covenant loyalty to Yahweh. They had committed spiritual adultery by defying God and marrying foreigners, and thus had "desecrated the sanctuary the LORD loves" (Mal 2:11).

In the process, of course, they had also broken faith with the "wife of your youth", with whom they were bound by marriage covenant. And they wondered why God was not responding to their tearful prayers! It was he who had made them one; and to break faith with one's wife (or "deal treacherously" as some translations put it), is an offence against him.

Since God unites a couple in marriage, he sees divorce as an act of violence against his work (2:16). He wants godly children, and he wants faithfulness in his people, because he is a faithful God. If a husband or wife cannot be faithful to his or her spouse, how can we be faithful to God? When divorce is an easy option, the value of faithfulness is diminished, and this in turn diminishes a person's perception of the faithfulness and dependability of God. We need to "guard ourselves in our spirit" (2:15-16), guard our commitments to our spouses, and keep faith with the God whose covenant with us endures forever.

Think it through

1. Do you think that people would describe you as a faithful person, one who keeps his or her word?

2. God calls us to be faithful to our marriage partners. If you are already married, what have you promised to do and to be for your spouse? What changes can you make to be more faithful to these promises?

3. If you're not yet married and intend to be at a later stage, what traits do you value highly for your future spouse?

Do you exhibit these traits yourself?

4. What parallels can you see between being a Christian and being married?

5. What implications does this study have for:

- 'trial' marriages (i.e. living together before marriage)?

- de facto marriages?

- marriage between a Christian and non-Christian?

5

Ready for justice

Injustice is frustrating; it is unbearable; it is tiresome. When aid money for war-torn countries is redirected into ammunition, or corrupt billionaires milk money out of the poor with dubious schemes, or a criminal escapes conviction through some legal technicality, we can be overwhelmed with a sense of futility. Will the perpetrators of evil never be brought to justice? Will the cycle of oppression never be broken?

The Israelites may have felt a similar sense of futility after their return from exile in Babylon. They had returned to Jerusalem with high hopes, only to be frustrated by poverty, famine, injustice and oppression (see study 2). The people of Judah were weary, so they complained to God. As we shall see, it turned out that God had the greater right to be weary.

Investigate
Read Malachi 2:17-3:18.

1. In what way have the Israelites wearied the Lord (2:17)?

2. What might have prompted the Israelites to say what they did?

3. God calls the Israelites to return to him (3:6-12). In what way have they left him?

4. What were the "harsh things" they have said about the Lord (vv. 13-15)?

Serving God—burdensome and futile?

The Israelites complained that the ungodly always seemed to triumph. Yet the reason that the blessings had not eventuated was their own behaviour. They were meant to bring the first 10% of their income to the temple, and they withheld it. Even so, it appears that they could not see that they were doing anything wrong.

What were they thinking when they claimed it was futile to obey God? Didn't the Israelites realize that they were accusing their Lord of being inconstant, withholding his blessing in spite of their "going about like mourners" (3:14)? They acted as if serving God was a painful burden, challenging his justice, kindness and generosity. It was a direct attack upon the character of God, and Yahweh rose wearily to his own defence.

Investigate

Look back over Malachi 2:17-3:18.

1. The Israelites asked, "Where is the God of justice?"(2:17). How does God explain his plan for justice (3:1-5)?

2. What will happen before the Lord comes to his temple?

3. What reason does God give for withholding his blessing from Israel (3:6-7)?

4. It is rare that God asks someone to test him (3:10). What does he call upon the Israelites to do as part of this test? What will be the outcome?

5. In answer to the question "Is it futile to serve God?" (3:14), the Lord reminds them about a day in the future. What will happen on this day?

6. Who are the people who will belong to the Lord? Why does the Lord choose them?

7. What will be the difference between these people, and those who complain to God?

God's coming justice

Israel complained about there being no justice, but that was exactly what was coming. God would send his messenger to prepare the way, and when they didn't expect it, the Lord himself would come. Yet his judgement wouldn't start with the pagans, but with the temple itself! This idea of commencing judgement with God's own people is repeated in the New Testament:

> … it is time for judgement to begin with the family of God;
> and if it begins with us, what will the outcome be for those
> who do not obey the gospel of God? (1 Pet 4:17)

We will talk more about the messenger in the next study, but we know that God has indeed come to his temple. Jesus cleansed the temple, prophesied its destruction and replaced it with his own death and resurrection, being himself the perfect sacrifice for sins for all time (Heb 10:10). This is made clear in John's gospel:

> Jesus answered them, "Destroy this temple, and I will raise
> it again in three days". The Jews replied, "It has taken forty-
> six years to build this temple, and you are going to raise it in
> three days?" But the temple he had spoken of was his body.
> (John 2:19-21)

We can no longer bring tithes to the temple because Jesus is our temple, but Malachi's message remains the same: return to God before the judgement comes.

We easily fall into the same trap as the Israelites. In a corrupt world where the unjust seem to prosper, we can find ourselves questioning whether in fact God is just. At those times we ought to heed the warning of Malachi and examine ourselves. We're not as innocent as we might think we are. In our prayerlessness, for example, we ignore God and his generosity, and when we do pray we often do so just to improve our own lot. Is it any wonder that God might hold back his blessings from us? By doing so he's sending us a clear message which we don't always want to hear. The message is for us to stop the evil that we're doing, and return to him.

The message is even more acute for Christians than it was to the Israelites. The messenger has come and the temple has been purified. All that now remains is the judgement day–the day when he will make us his own treasured possession, his own people whom he has chosen out. Evil will be destroyed on that day, but his own people will be saved. On that day his people will see clearly the difference between the righteous (those who serve God) and the wicked (those who do not).

Think it through

1. Make a list of some of the good things that you have in life. Can you see God's kind provision in these things?

2. The Israelites stole from God. We may not steal in the usual sense, but are we thieves in a more general sense? For example:

    • Have you thought through your giving to Christian work?

    • Do you work diligently for your employer?

    • Do you pay the appropriate tax to the government?

    • Do you respect copyright laws concerning books, music and computer games?

    Discuss how you might deal with some of these areas.

3. In study 3, we considered whether we offer God our whole lives. In what ways might failure to do so be a kind of stealing?

4. Are there things in your life that may cause God to withhold his blessings?

5. What encouragement has this study given us for the times we find it burdensome to wait for justice to come?

6. Are you yourself ready for the day of his coming?

The dawn of that Day

When life is going well, it's hard to look forward to heaven. Those who live in prosperous and peaceful societies may wonder why we would want anything else. But for those who know oppression, injustice and hardship, the promise of a better future is met with eager anticipation. As we have seen, that was Malachi's experience. He longed for the day of prosperity which the prophets had proclaimed. The eager expectation of that day is evident in the powerful imagery of the last chapter of Malachi.

Investigate

Read Malachi 4:1-6.

1. The coming day is described in terms of a fire. What does this fire have in store for the wicked?

2. What will the righteous do on that day?

3. Before this, God will send his messenger. Read Isaiah 40:1-5, and describe what had already been revealed before Malachi's time about the preparation for the Lord's coming.

4. What do we learn about the messenger in Malachi 4?

5. Read the following passages, and see if the events described correspond with what was expected of God's messenger.

   • Matthew 11:7-11

   • Matthew 11:12-15

Looking to the past

Some people live for the present. They keep right up to date with the trends and fads of culture, always changing to meet the latest expectation. Others pursue the future, consulting astrologers and mediums (even economists!) to try to find out what is in store, or to change what is in store.

Christians need to be people of the past. This doesn't mean we must be old-fashioned, or frightened of change; it means that God has *already revealed* in the past what will happen in the future, and that is the place we ought to look for direction.

Malachi called Israel back to what Moses said at Mt Horeb (Mt Sinai), on the edge of the promised land, when God gave him the law and explained what it meant to be one of his people. God gave them two choices—live his way and receive his blessings, or reject God and have him curse the land, livestock and children (Deut 30).

One of the commandments that God gave the people on that day was the command to "Honour you father and your mother, so that you may live long in the land the LORD your God is giving you" (Exod 20:12). Honouring your parents as an Israelite would create a 'trail of honour' reaching back to Abraham and the covenant promises God had made to him. By contrast, the people of Israel had moved so far away from the covenant of their forefathers, that their forefathers wouldn't recognize them!

The first ray of dawn

In 1 and 2 Kings, Elijah the prophet called the people back to their covenant with God. The 'new' Elijah referred to in Malachi 4:5 was to fulfil the same role. By calling them back, he would prepare them for the judgement day. The new Elijah was the first ray of the dawn of the new age. Jesus told us in Matthew 11 that this new Elijah, the messenger who was to come, was none other than John the Baptist. John fulfilled the prophecies of both Malachi and Isaiah. He knew his task—to announce the coming of the Lord, his kingdom and his judgement, and to call for repentance. John's baptism recognized repentance, but just as being a physical descendant of Abraham wasn't enough to belong to Israel, so being baptized wasn't enough to find forgiveness. People were to repent and turn back to the faith that their father Abraham had.

So how did they receive God's messenger?

Investigate

1. Read Matthew 21:23-32.

    a. Jesus answered the Pharisees' question by asking another question. Why did his question give the Pharisees so much difficulty?

    b. What was the difference between the two sons in the parable?

    c. What do you think is the point of the parable?

    d. How does this parable relate to John the Baptist?

2. Read Luke 7:24-35. What is the error of the Pharisees?

3. What was John the Baptist's fate (see Matt 14:1-12)?

Living in the Day of the Lord

John the Baptist's work was the same as Elijah's—to turn people back to the faith of Abraham, Isaac and Jacob, back to the faith of the Scriptures. John prepared the way for Jesus by calling for repentance. Those who repented then welcomed the Lord Jesus, and those who didn't, rejected him.

We now live in the Day of the Lord, the day that was ushered in by Jesus' resurrection. We're only in the dawn of that day—we see its first light in the salvation we know in Christ. We feel its warmth, but the fierce heat of the day is still to come. Those who fear the Lord will bask in that warmth, but the wicked will become like ashes (Mal 4:3). To God's people, the sun will be like a marvellous bird "risen with healing in its wings" and we will respond like delighted calves who have been set free to relish the day! To those who have not repented, that same rising sun destroys them in judgement.

Christianity offers the real hope of a changed life, and a new day of righteousness when justice will finally be done. The prophecy of Malachi reminds us that in order to experience God's blessing on that day, we must turn back to God. If our lives are going well, if we think we're probably good enough to keep God happy and we can't really understand why God would be angry with us, then we will not want to repent. Who needs such a demanding God?

Malachi is a warning that God remembers those who fear and honour his name, and who have now found salvation in Christ.

All others are destined for destruction. Let us find the forgiveness of God in the death of Jesus, and repent of our old ways. As the apostle Paul wrote to the Ephesians:

> Surely you heard of him and were taught in him in accordance with the truth that is in Jesus. You were taught, with regard to your former way of life, to put off your old self, which is being corrupted by its deceitful desires; to be made new in the attitude of your minds; and to put on the new self, created to be like God in true righteousness and holiness. (Eph 4:21-24)

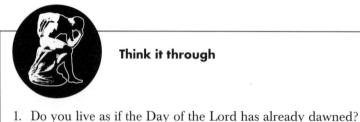

Think it through

1. Do you live as if the Day of the Lord has already dawned?

2. Have you made the step of repenting and asking God for forgiveness? If not, what things stand in your way, and why?

3. If God has revealed his plans in the past, what should be our attitude towards the Bible?

4. "The fact that there is injustice in the world proves that there isn't a God." How would you reply to such a statement?

5. How does your old self compare with your new self? Are there aspects of your old self still present that you should address?

6. Summarize the things that have been particularly striking to you through this set of 6 studies.

- In terms of God's plans and Israel's response:

- In terms of how we should live now:

Matthias Media is a ministry team of like-minded, evangelical Christians working together to achieve a particular goal, as summarized in our mission statement:

> *To serve our Lord Jesus Christ, and the growth of his gospel in the world, by producing and delivering high quality, Bible-based resources.*

It was in 1988 that we first started pursuing this mission together, and in God's kindness we now have more than 250 different ministry resources being distributed all over the world. These resources range from Bible studies and books, through to training courses and audio sermons.

To find out more about our large range of very useful products, and to access samples and free downloads, visit our website:

www.matthiasmedia.com.au

How to buy our resources

1. Direct from us over the internet:
    – in the US: www.matthiasmedia.com
    – in Australia and the rest of the world: www.matthiasmedia.com.au

2. Direct from us by phone:
    – in the US: 1 866 407 4530
    – in Australia: 1800 814 360 (Sydney: 9663 1478)
    – international: +61-2-9663-1478

3. Through a range of outlets in various parts of the world. Visit **www.matthiasmedia.com.au/international.php** for details about recommended retailers in your part of the world, including www.thegoodbook.co.uk in the United Kingdom.

4. Trade enquiries can be addressed to:
    – in the US: sales@matthiasmedia.com
    – in the UK: sales@ivpbooks.com
    – in Australia and the rest of the world: sales@matthiasmedia.com.au

Other Interactive and Topical Bible Studies from Matthias Media:

Our Interactive Bible Studies (IBS) and Topical Bible Studies (TBS) are a valuable resource to help you keep feeding from God's Word. The IBS series works through passages and books of the Bible; the TBS series pulls together the Bible's teaching on topics such as money or prayer. As at April 2008, the series contains the following titles:

BEYOND EDEN
(GENESIS 1-11)
Authors: Phillip Jensen and Tony Payne, 9 studies

OUT OF DARKNESS
(EXODUS 1-18)
Author: Andrew Reid, 8 studies

THE ONE AND ONLY
(DEUTERONOMY)
Author: Bryson Smith, 8 studies

THE GOOD, THE BAD & THE UGLY
(JUDGES)
Author: Mark Baddeley, 10 studies

FAMINE & FORTUNE
(RUTH)
Authors: Barry Webb and David Höhne, 4 studies

RENOVATOR'S DREAM
(NEHEMIAH)
Authors: Phil Campbell and Greg Clarke, 7 studies

THE EYE OF THE STORM
(JOB)
Author: Bryson Smith, 6 studies

THE SEARCH FOR MEANING
(ECCLESIASTES)
Author: Tim McMahon, 9 studies

TWO CITIES
(ISAIAH)
Authors: Andrew Reid and Karen Morris, 9 studies

KINGDOM OF DREAMS
(DANIEL)
Authors: Andrew Reid and Karen Morris, 9 studies

BURNING DESIRE
(OBADIAH & MALACHI)
Authors: Phillip Jensen and Richard Pulley, 6 studies

WARNING SIGNS
(JONAH)
Author: Andrew Reid, 6 studies

FULL OF PROMISE
(THE BIG PICTURE OF THE O.T.)
Authors: Phil Campbell and Bryson Smith, 8 studies

THE GOOD LIVING GUIDE
(MATTHEW 5:1-12)
Authors: Phillip Jensen and Tony Payne, 9 studies

NEWS OF THE HOUR
(MARK)
Author: Peter Bolt, 10 studies

MISSION UNSTOPPABLE
(ACTS)
Author: Bryson Smith, 10 studies

THE FREE GIFT OF LIFE
(ROMANS 1-5)
Author: Gordon Cheng, 8 studies

THE FREE GIFT OF SONSHIP
(ROMANS 6-11)
Author: Gordon Cheng, 8 studies

PROCLAIMING THE RISEN LORD
(LUKE 24-ACTS 2)
Author: Peter Bolt, 6 studies

FREE FOR ALL
(GALATIANS)
Authors: Phillip Jensen and Kel Richards, 8 studies

WALK THIS WAY
(EPHESIANS)
Author: Bryson Smith, 8 studies

PARTNERS FOR LIFE
(PHILIPPIANS)
Author: Tim Thorburn, 8 studies

THE COMPLETE CHRISTIAN
(COLOSSIANS)
Authors: Phillip Jensen and Tony Payne, 8 studies

TO THE HOUSEHOLDER
(1 TIMOTHY)
Authors: Phillip Jensen and Greg Clarke, 9 studies

RUN THE RACE
(2 TIMOTHY)
Author: Bryson Smith, 6 studies

THE PATH TO GODLINESS
(TITUS)
Authors: Phillip Jensen and Tony Payne, 6 studies

FROM SHADOW TO REALITY
(HEBREWS)
Author: Joshua Ng, 10 studies

THE IMPLANTED WORD
(JAMES)
Authors: Phillip Jensen and Kirsten Birkett, 8 studies

HOMEWARD BOUND
(1 PETER)
Authors: Phillip Jensen and Tony Payne, 10 studies

ALL YOU NEED TO KNOW
(2 PETER)
Author: Bryson Smith, 6 studies

THE VISION STATEMENT
(REVELATION)
Author: Greg Clarke, 9 studies

BOLD I APPROACH
(PRAYER)
Author: Tony Payne, 6 studies

CASH VALUES
(MONEY)
Author: Tony Payne, 5 studies

THE BLUEPRINT
(DOCTRINE)
Authors: Phillip Jensen and Tony Payne, 11 studies

WOMAN OF GOD
(THE BIBLE ON WOMEN)
Author: Terry Blowes, 8 studies

Notes

Notes

Notes

Notes